Passing Through the Fire

A Woman's Diary

Rose A. Juma

authorHOUSE®

AuthorHouse™
1663 Liberty Drive
Bloomington, IN 47403
www.authorhouse.com
Phone: 1-800-839-8640

First published by AuthorHouse 1/21/2010

ISBN: 978-1-4490-0091-2 (sc)

Printed in the United States of America
Bloomington, Indiana

This book is printed on acid-free paper.

Contents

INTRODUCTION

Written in a fiction format, this book is intended for those women going through very heart breaking experiences in the name of love and marriage. Some of these women are married to men of different characters that can be dangerous to their own well being even when their spouse's intention is well meant.

Due to their faithfulness to their marriages, or for fear of what the society will say; cultural and traditional beliefs or even religious beliefs, these women end up staying in these relationships or marriages, persevering through all sorts of heartbreaking experiences endlessly.

Fear of moving children from one relationship to another might be a hard decision to make.

This book is based on a real life story. The names of the characters have been changed for security reasons. Some place names have been changed while others have remained for reasons of making the story authentic.

The Author believes that there is no situation too hard for God and He will always make a way. It is however, her hope that when the Spirit of the LORD speaks to us, that we will be able to hear and act accordingly.

May God's Grace and Mercy be with you as you read this book.

Amen!

NO ONE CAN HOLD YOU BACK

"Oh God, help me, I cannot take it anymore!!! Charles, this is it. I cannot take it any longer."

That was what I told Carolina. It was what I felt. I was tired of this whole life with Charles. After taking a deep breath and a sigh that seemed to come from deep within, Carolina said,

"Dianne there is still hope. Nobody can hold you back but you. Nothing is impossible with God. It might seem impossible to man, as though you have reached a dead end, but believe me, you are passing through the fire, you are being purged, and when you come out of it, when the fire dies out, you will have a testimony."

Carolina could find hope and encouragement in any desperate situation. She was older and so she is the one I turned to whenever I needed that wisdom that comes with life's experience. She had a calm Spirit, a prayerful woman of God. The kind of woman whose life looks so perfect like nothing has ever really happened in her life. She possessed the confidence and credibility of having been through it and done it all. What with thirty and twenty eight year old sons, and two grand children, and yet looking so young, one would think she had just turned thirty. You could feel that her credibility was genuine and authentic. That is why I was pouring my heart out to her, this particular day.

I desperately cried out, "What do you mean nobody can hold me back but me, when I have been held back all these years? And what kind of fire is this that burns endlessly? It has been burning none stop for the last ten years, Carolina I cannot take it anymore."

"Let me ask you," I continued, opening up wounds that I never would have shared with anybody until now. "Is God really seeing what I have been through all these years?

"Oh yes He does," Carolina's quick response cut me short. "Remember Job and his afflictions? God saw it all and remember, He never allowed anything to touch his soul."

Daring to measure my afflictions to those of Job's, I headed straight to every temptation I had gone through and continued,

"I have felt like Job in the Bible in so many occasions. It all started in 1987, one morning when Charles told me, almost in a whisper.

"Uncle Dominic and Aunt Felicia are coming to stay with us"

"Why?" I had asked.

"I told them that we were having difficulty paying the rent, so they said, they were willing to have our house, but before they take it up, we could stay together and share the rent payment. We could stay with them until we got ourselves a smaller apartment, I thought it was fine" Charles replied.

I didn't see any problem with that, so I had said "That is fine."

I had married Charles just seven months ago and then he had lost his job. So this conversation was taking place three months after he lost his job, and I could not afford to pay the US$ 1,500 rent, for the house.

From the onset of our relationship with Charles, something was wrong, but blinded by love, I did not see it. I had loved him so much to see any fault in his finances and expenditure. During this conversation, I was two months pregnant with our first child.

True to their word, Uncle Dominic and Aunt Felicia came and stayed with us. We were living in a middle class suburb. Later, I learnt from Charles' parents that, it was not in order for an older man to stay in his younger brother's house; but we were innocent and did not know a thing about culture, being Christians; we were not under the law because Christ had redeemed us from the curse of the Law. If Uncle Dominic and Aunt Felicia knew about it but kept quiet, no one knows.

Our life together was very difficult. I really don't know why, maybe it was jealous, but what I know is that, much of the tension was created by the fact that it was Felicia's brother, one of the Directors of the company that Charles had worked for, that had terminated Charles' services. So there was really no trust between us. I had my personal fears, I thought that since Felicia had not been blessed with children of her own, for the past twelve years they had been married and that I was only seven months married and already expected our first baby might have been something that made me not trust her. I really couldn't pin down the wrong thing but things were not just right. A stranger could have walked in and felt it in the atmosphere. The presence of God was not in the house anymore.

So our life was such that, I never ate what she prepared and I rarely sat in my living room anymore to watch television although it was my favorite pass time. We rarely talked to each other apart from greetings. We were married to the two brothers and yet had no ties; whether this affected the brothers or not, I was not aware of. Felicia could travel a lot for reasons known to herself, not even her husband Dominic knew where she traveled to.

Felicia was a tall lady in her late forties. She was slim and with a light skin. Her smile was usually what I called a grin rather than a smile. It was obvious that something was bothering her but she seemed to be in control of the situation. She drank a lot of alcohol, I guess to help her forget her worries. Finances were not her problem. She had an Administrative position which she also supplemented with an Import/Export business of her own. These two jobs paid her well. Her brother Bill who had terminated Charles' services was the Director of a very successful company, and was very close to her. So her problems were basically other than financial.

Dominic, her husband and my brother in-law, was very dark and plump. He never seemed to be in control of the situation, especially finances. If one happened to ask him for a five dollar bill, or to buy groceries for the house, he would ask it from the wife. If one did not know how things were between them, it was easy to assume that he was a mean man, but he was following the strict rules from the wife, she was the "Commander in Chief." Remember, it was her brother who was the "director."

We all just called them Uncle Dominic and Aunt Felicia.

On one occasion, I remember aunt Felicia had traveled. She had prepared a meal and left the food on the gas cooker. She never knew how much I cared less for food during the pregnancy. I think she only realized it when after one week she came back to find that the food and the pan were untouched. I never trusted her; this lack of trust does not just come from nowhere. It is like the spirit warning you, giving you a red light to watch out. It just feels like a deep rooted thing in there. I believe Job had this feeling when he said, for the thing which I greatly feared is come upon me, and that which I was afraid of is come unto me (Job 3:25). It is our instinct or the sixth sense to warn us of the looming dangers or happenings that we may not see with our naked eye.

One day, out of the blues, Aunt Felicia came with a truck and moved away all their household from the house. Furniture, Shrank, pots and pans, name it, she took everything. It was nothing to do with anybody, and not even Uncle Dominic knew where she was going. However, as we learnt later she had moved out to marry another man as a second wife. She stayed there for five years only to come back.

It is at this time that the reality of our situation dawned on me. Charles had never been able to buy a bed for us. We had been using one of the very many beds Aunt Felicia had all this time and I did not know. So when things were very bad, the bed was taken by its owner.

After this, the rest followed like a domino effect. Call it a stronghold or a curse or was it a punishment for a wrong done? Thinking of Job's friends in the Bible, I even started searching my heart if I had done something wrong and God was punishing me or us. Thank God I know better today than then.

After this of course we could not continue to live in this big house; we had to get an alternative immediately without any delay. The first alternative of cost-sharing had failed, so we had to get another option. Moving to a smaller apartment was the only answer to this puzzle. We found one within the same area. One of our neighbors had been looking for a house and so we moved in to her apartment and she moved into our house. It was a one room apartment.

In this new apartment, things were not very amusing. Our television had been earlier on re-possessed by the shop for lack of payment. We now had no bed to sleep on. My pregnancy problems were there to reckon with. Our furniture could not fit in the small room. We had to spread our beddings down on the floor and partition the section with a curtain. As though this was not enough, I felt an unusual uneasiness in the atmosphere. There was something not quite right. I just felt it.

At this point Carolina cut me short, "what do you mean you just felt it? You were opening a door with your fears, you just quoted Job to me, don't you see that you somehow opened a door and the enemy used it as he wanted to?"

"Oh, well, at that particular time I did not know anything about opening doors with my fears, no one had taught me about opening doors with my thoughts, I did not know about confession and lining my thoughts with what the Word of God says." I replied.

"Well, go ahead" Carolina encouraged me.

Well, one day, our new landlord came, we had never met him and that was our first encounter with him. Surprisingly he demanded that we pay rent for that month. We were shocked because the person we exchanged houses with had told us that she had paid the rent for the month. We had paid our rent from the previous house and had moved with that understanding and confirmed everything before the actual movement.

The landlord was not ready to reason with us. He was not even ready to wait for us to settle the matter with the former occupant, he told us to move immediately. This explains the emptiness I felt around the house when we had just moved in. The devourer was working overtime on our lives.

This apartment had looked like a jammed storage, with no organization at all. Being in my seventh month pregnancy did not help either. Things had changed so fast I could not take it all at once and it was hard to cope. I felt like Job in the Bible, as he received the sad news about his children, asses, and everything he had been blessed with being killed, stolen and destroyed in a twinkle of an eye. I was still going to work with no place to live in, I had to think of what my new born baby would wear, eat and sleep on. My husband Charles had no penny to his name. I had to pay the rent to the unknown place we would move to, and on top of that buy food. My pay was not enough at all; however, because I married love and not wealth as I normally put it, I was fine. The word of God according to 1Corinthians 13:7 told me that love, "beareth all things, believeth all things, hopeth all things and endureth all things. And that Love is patient. During this harsh time, I comforted myself by replacing the word Love with my name Dianne, and used to say, Dianne beareth all things, Dianne believeth all things, hopeth all things and endureth all things. Dianne is patient. This made things seem bearable.

It became apparent that we had to move again only two weeks after our first move. So one day, as I came from work Charles told me that he had found an apartment in a housing project. This was a very bad neighborhood in terms of security, but at least Charles was in control of the situation at least for now and he had found a place for his little family. So we moved, later in the years to follow, it was going to be different I would be the one to look for houses or apartments to move to.

If I thought that the one roomed apartment we had for the two weeks was small, I was in for a rude shock. In the housing project, I was going to come face to face with the bitter truth of poverty. You know the thief cometh not but for to steal, to kill and to destroy but I am (Jesus) come that they might have life and that they might have it more abundantly, (John 10:10). Like Job I felt things slipping away very fast, the only difference was that this was real and it was happening to me, I was not reading it in a book.

The first thing that hit me was that the bathrooms and the toilets were communal, they were outside. Apart from that, even the sink for washing dishes was outside. We had to share all these important, intimate basic necessities with a hoard of about twelve other families not to mention the number of members in each family.

This was a life I had never lived in my maiden life. It was not easy to come to terms with such life and I never accepted it. It was a dissatisfying status quo that I just refused to accept was my portion. Most of the time, I defiantly locked myself up in my apartment, rarely being seen outside. I felt as though I was necked and everybody could see my nakedness. The only place I felt comfortable was in the "castle of my skin."

My baby was born in this circumstance. The conditions in which he entered into the world were far from what I had dreamt of. Of course, by this time I had known that I could not afford a private hospital, but for one to have told me that some new born babies slept down on the floor with their mothers in any hospital in any country's National Hospital, was not anything I had expected.

Well, on this particular day, I went to the hospital due to loss of fluid. Before the delivery, the doctors and the interns were all over me and kept on checking on all of the patients as frequent as possible. However, after delivery, and especially if the delivery turned out to be a normal one with no complications, then the patients' delicate care by the doctors was over. One was left at the mercies of the nurses. Nurses have never been very kind though; it is just something about that profession, some can be very mean.

I delivered my baby at around 11:00 pm. I was dumped on a bench, and never knew where my baby was. I felt nauseated and tired. I was left on that bench till the wee hours of the morning. Some of the women were seated next to me carrying their babies on the bench; I was too weak to carry mine. In the wee hours of the morning, my baby was brought to me and we were led to a ward. We were about ten women filing behind each other, with our babies on our hands. The situation was pathetic, some had blood flowing down their legs and as we walked traces of blood filled the floor. As we came to the ward, I realized that all the beds were occupied I was directed to share one bed with my baby and another woman also with her baby. Goodness!! What on earth was going on? Yes, I knew I was on the very low level of the social status, but to share a one small 3x6 bed with a fellow woman, each one of us with her baby was incredible.

If I thought this was bad enough, I must have counted myself blessed just a few minutes later, because the rest of the women and yet another group of women were ushered in to the same ward and were not so fortunate to find a bed to share with one another. They had to spread their own – (for a lack of a better word) wrappers on the floor, to sleep on with their new born babies, all that the hospital provided for them was some canvases which were spread on the floor; however, these were very few that those who missed them had to do with whatever cloth they had carried along with them from home.

I swear to my God, if anyone had told me that this was happening in the Country's National Hospital, I would have thought he was spreading negative rumors against the country I loved. However this was not told to me, I experienced it personally. All my dreams of ever having a luxurious bed with my new born baby sleeping in a different bed were shattered. It was really a painful experience. This is where I think my attitude towards Charles began to be affected, although the tale-tells had been there during the difficult period of the nine months.

I didn't take long in the hospital. One day was just enough. Back home there was totally no food at all. Charles left shortly to go to his cousin somewhere in the neighborhood and by the time he came back, I had already spread the mattress and the beddings on the floor ready to sleep.

One thing I must mention here about this one roomed apartment is that, it was really small. All of our belongings were placed on top of each other. The room was always dark and lights had to be left on throughout the day to provide some light in the house. There was no space for any permanent bedding let alone for the whole sofa-set. So during the day, my baby slept on the seat and at night we moved things up and down to make our beddings.

Being the loving, submissive wife, and now a mother that I was, I still had hope and trusted that this was not my life and that one of these days; Charles was going to do something to move us out of this mess, this was temporary.

So when he came up with these lucrative ideas of me taking up some loan for him to help him start some business, I thought wow! At long last, he was doing something. I have to mention at this point, that, even from the word go; our relationship initially had begun when Charles had involved me in a loan affair which I did not know what it was meant for. He was my fiancé, so I did not really ask why he was requesting me to take up a loan for him.

So at this particular time, what I did not know then, was the cautious saying that "when the plan looks too good to be true think twice." I trusted him and had faith that he would do what he said he wanted the money for. And hoped that it would subsequently, take us out of this mess and into our dream life. What I did not know was that, this was going to be the trend all my life with Charles.

Anyway, I applied for a loan of US$ 15,000 and gave it all to him; never did I use even a single cent for a cup of coffee. I did not want to mess up the plans lest he would be short. He had to have enough. That is what love does. "trusteth all things." Well that was in 1985, to this date, as I sit writing this book, I do not know what happened to the whole amount of US $ 15,000, but I know, I paid it all back plus the interest through the monthly deductions. One thing I know though, that the anxiety I had, to find out what had happened to this money or the project it was meant to do, caused lots and lots of tension between us. Our communication started becoming sour each day. There was a rift building between us. Bitterness filled our apartment and we acted as strangers towards each other.

By early 1989, I feared the marriage was not going to last. I wrote a letter to Charles telling him my fears. In reply instead of telling me what was happening with the project I took the loan for, he said that he really did not know how I expected him to take all the abuses I had hurled at him.

Sure I had been frustrated with lack of communication and just being informed of the developments. I was bitter and had been demanding answers to all the questions about the project, but he never said anything about it. I felt sorry and realized how hard I had been and all the pain I had

11

caused him with the abuses I had hurled at him. I apologized and we became a happy family once again full of hope and energy to tackle this misfortune together.

However, this was just on the surface, the reality was that at the back of my conscience, an eleven months marriage to a jobless husband, who took money from me and never bothered to discuss anything about it, was quite disturbing and unbearable.

After this episode, I started job hunting for him. It became a routine, having his application letters, and resumes typed by my mother and then taking them to prospective employers on his behalf. All this I did in the hope that I was helping him concentrate on the development of setting up the business project. It is over twenty years now and nothing has come out of it.

Well, today I feel that there was a lot of my running around up and down for Charles that I forgot myself. Something lied to me that only a man could change a woman's social and economical status. It was much later that I realized how wrong I was. In those years I could accompany Charles to the cooperative building for his export/import business, in which he tried his hands on. I could check on his appointments for job promises. I prayed for him more than I prayed for myself. I became all that I thought a supportive wife should be.

As though I never knew the saying, once bitten twice shy," I let Charles talk me into helping him with yet some other funds. This trend went on and on and the amounts he needed from me went on increasing. It started with US$ 15,000. It then moved to US$ 30,000 and then to other small ones, that when put together would add up to US$ 1,000,000 considering the interest all these debts accrued and I paid them all. They were all bits and pieces some from my friends; others involved repayment of his "rent-to-own" television sets, all in the name of trying his hands on some business that would eventually take us out of the situation we were in. Then in 1990..."

All of a sudden, I caught myself and realized that I was telling Carolina everything that I had been holding in my heart, the unforgiveness and blame I had carried all these ten years towards Charles. I had hated all men because Charles had failed me. I was a bitter woman and blamed it all on Charles. Now I was not sure I wanted to open up anymore. So I suddenly stopped.

Carolina asked, "Why did you suddenly stop?" "Go on" she encouraged.

"No" I replied. I feel guilty. Why am I opening up to you anyway? I have been safe in my cocoon all these years, acting as though all is well. Doesn't the Bible say "in everything give thanks, for this is the will of God in Christ Jesus concerning you? (1Thesalonians 5:18) and anyway I feel more secure that way." I continued.

"No Dianne," Carolina retorted. Don't misuse the word of God because you are in bitterness. The same word of God says in Mark 11:25, "And when you stand praying, forgive if you have ought against any: that your Father also which is in heaven may forgive you your trespasses. But if you do not forgive, neither will your Father which is in heaven forgive you your trespasses." And you sound as though you really need to do some forgiving. It is this unforgiveness that is binding you up; unforgiveness is a bondage in itself. So go ahead and do exactly what God requires Christians to do; repenting. Getting it out of your heart and saying God, this burden is too heavy for me. Please take it away."

She then added, Remember when Daniel the prophet was in prayer and fasting, repenting his sins and those of Israel? That's what you are doing right now." You are repenting both your sins and Charles' right now.

"Are you sure this is not complaining," I questioned, "remember what happened to the children of Israel when they complained and murmured against Moses, I don't want to be complaining against Charles"

"No."Carolina said, "it is crying out to God in surrender for Him to help you just like God said about Israel while they were in Egypt, I have heard the cry of my People…"

"And in your own words, you are crying out to God" she went on, (reminding me of how this whole conversation started.) "Oh God, help me, I cannot take it anymore."

"God will release the burden removing, yoke destroying anointing upon you," Carolina continued. "You are crying out to God right now, and laying it all down at the cross. He is looking inside your heart right now and seeing that broken heart and as Isaiah 61:1-3 says,

"The Spirit of the Lord is upon me; because the LORD hath anointed me to preach good tidings unto the meek; He hath sent me to bind up the broken hearted, to proclaim liberty to the captives, and the opening of the prison to them that are bound; To proclaim the acceptable year of the LORD and the day of vengeance of our God; to comfort all that mourn; to appoint unto them that mourn in Zion, to give them beauty for ashes, the oil of joy for mourning, the garment of praise for the spirit of heaviness; that they might be called the trees of righteousness, the planting of the LORD, that he might be glorified." (Isaiah 61:1-3) and He wants to do that for you right now. You need healing Dianne."

"Refer back to Mark 11:25-26, He says, and when you stand praying forgive...but if ye do not forgive, neither will your Father which is in heaven forgive your trespasses?

So you have to get it out of your chest and repent and surrender to Him, and He will surely forgive and heal you. This is a healing process for both of you. You have been holding both of you, no wonder nothing has ever changed all these years, you are just going in circles in the same spot." Carolina concluded her sermon.

"mmhh" I sighed feeling encouraged. Something was really happening. If there was anything I wanted to do, was save my marriage that was now in shambles, and if Carolina was right, I needed to forgive Charles. If that was the door for the miracle, I was willing to try it.

"O.k. where was I?" I asked, feeling some encouragement, like I was doing the right thing, determined to have it done with.

"1990..." Carolina reminded me.

1990

"You have to move out today if you cannot pay me the whole amount." My Landlord said.

"I promise to pay you." I pleaded, not knowing where I would get the money from. In my mind, I knew this was a dry promise. How many such promises had I made to him without fulfilling any of them?

"No," the man retorted, "I cannot accept these lies any longer, you keep on paying your rent in bits and you have never been able to pay it all. I am tired, get out I want to lock my apartment and rent it out to some other tenant who is able to pay." He screamed at the top of his voice.

By then we had moved to several apartments and this might have been the tenth one. It was always the same story. I was then a student at the College. Charles totally had nothing to do. He could not place his hands on anything and succeed. He was so hopeless and helpless.

That evening, the landlord had come with three other people to actually throw us out of the apartment. Throw us out with all our belongings. Our belongings meant, one stool, a table, a few utensils, a bed and lots of papers and files tied in boxes.

When a landlord comes to throw a tenant out, they are merciless. As soon as he gave the men the order, they threw everything, all I saw were things flying through the door. They were worthless things, by this time, we had nothing valuable. If we had, the landlord would have taken them to make up for the accumulated rent payments. Things had turned out that I was now responsible for the rent payment. I had been unable to pay it considering the loan repayment that Charles had made me take for him in the hope of succeeding in some business; the rent had accumulated to a total of US$ 800. The only valuable item we had was an electrical iron box, and he took that away with him.

That night we had no choice but to sleep outside in the open. I curled my son closer to me and my house help next to me. Charles lay on the side. We actually fell asleep the whole night, and only formed a feast to the mosquitoes.

In the morning, Charles went away and took so long. I thought he would be back with some great idea of where to move his family to. When he did not come back by midday, my mind started thinking. I was devastated. What was I to do, were we going to spend another night outside again? God please help me, I cried.

God actually gave me an Idea. Opposite our apartment, there was an incomplete building totally unoccupied by anyone. It was bushy and deserted. I went into one of the rooms and cleaned it and put my young house-help and my son into it. Surprisingly, I was not afraid, I felt like God speaking to me through Joshua and saying, Do not be afraid, every place that the sole of your foot shall tread upon that have I given unto you, as I said unto Moses. I had this courage of a surviving lioness seeking for shelter for her cubs. We were the only people in the quarter among five empty apartments, supposedly occupied with all sorts of insects and snakes. Thieves had also broken into all of them and had stolen all the windows, so what I had were just window frames. I took cartons and used them to block the wind for that night; there were three windows in total.

That night, Charles came back as though everything had been normal. He had no solution to the problem, so we all slept in this new "apartment." The next day, I even got more creative and adventurers; I cleaned another smaller apartment because the one we were in had been bigger and the wind had blown right inside. This time I selected one that had only one window and was therefore not so windy. Despite the fact that it had no window glasses, and the door lock had been stolen, it proved to be warmer.

God was and still is good to me. We managed to stay in that house for a whole year, not paying any rent and with nobody knocking at my door asking for rent and sending me packing. Jehovah Jireh provided for a roof over our head for a whole year. At this time I was still repaying the loan I had taken for Charles, I was a student at the college and needed bus fare and money to feed the family every day. These were totally up to me.

COLLEGE LIFE

"Dianne, why have you deteriorated in your class performance? I am concerned, because you always come to class late, is everything alright? The head of the Department of Information and Liberal studies once asked me.

I was frank, and told him that I was going through a difficult time because my husband had lost his job and was not helping me. It was difficult for me to manage everything.

And what this meant was that, I had to find out in the morning, how I was to leave my family with food before I left. I had to ask for bus fare everyday from I did not know who. I had to think seriously on how to get to college and back home on a daily basis. At times my fellow classmates helped me, but sometimes I had to approach total strangers. These total strangers later became friends that would always help me more often. What I can only say here is that God provides to His children in a miraculous way.

Whenever the college closed for holidays, I was supposed to go back to the office to work. But I reasoned that since I was on payroll that did not help me much; I needed to do some extra jobs to get some extra cash on me. So, during the holidays, I called the office and said I had some research work to carry out and that I needed time to do it. This sufficed.

So I did a lot of part time jobs. These jobs later turned out to give me a lot of experience and exposure that I needed. I would like to think of them today as internships, only they were paid. Some of them were actually within the Department I worked for which paid me an extra US$ 600 per week. This proved quite helpful for the much needed cash for my family. It subsidized my US$ 150, which had been my net pay for years now. Thanks be to God.

Such jobs were not forthcoming all the year round. There was one time I did not get any such jobs at all. And since I had to feed my family, I decided to sell vegetables to cope.

At one point I also got an extra administrative work that paid me US$ 2000. This was great. It happened that the place I went to look for a part time job, belonged to a man that had previously been a total stranger. And as I mentioned before, these total strangers later became friends. So when I went to see him to ask for a part-time job, it happened that he was in need of an administrative assistant. He needed more hands to help in the data entry of a directory he was publishing. And since we had met before, he took me on and I joined the busy crew with data entry.

Well, I managed to complete my certificate course in Library and information studies. I was determined to get a promotion back at the office. I also had a deep desire to further pursue my librarianship profession. My promotion took time. It depended on various things. First, it depended on the availability of the Library Assistant position. Secondly, the priority list of all the qualified librarians within the Department of health had to be considered.

It turned out, that if I was transferred to the Medical Training College Library, I would stand a better chance of promotion. My second baby came at this time before my transfer.

All through the nine months period, it had proved to be a very difficult pregnancy emotionally, I was scared, I did not know how I was going to cope. I was not able to feed just one baby, how was I going to manage to support two of them. I had hoped that the pills I was on would have helped until I completed my professional studies and have good footing before another baby. Where would it sleep? I was still sleeping with my first baby on our bed although he was two and a half years. What would it eat or wear? I had wondered, all through this pregnancy. Being overtaken by the cares of the world I had forgotten the Word in Mathew 6:34 that urge us to "Take therefore no thought for the morrow: for the morrow shall take thought for the things of itself. Sufficient unto the day is the evil thereof." Instead I succumbed to the cares and worries over my coming baby.

Due to all these thoughts and worries about the bleak future I was bringing my baby into, I kept on being sickly. Twice I was hospitalized, I was anemic, and had malaria, the baby was depressed, even to the day she was born. I was so weak since I never ate properly during the pregnancy. I went through it all by the mercies of God.

Anyway, I thank God for this lovely girl. She makes me very proud and gives me a reason to live. Both my children were conceived in love and joy. And no matter the circumstances surrounding their birth, they have given me patience and focus to keep on going.

1991

Somewhere in the late 1991, due to the fact that I had a Certificate in Librarianship, I had been posted to the National's Medical Training College Library. I felt good. I thought, I needed to make some new furniture to uplift the look of my house to crown my joy.

Charles had been trying his hand on furniture business. He taught himself carpentry and at times he would make an item and sell it and this helped in the house. I got some money; it was an arrears payment of some kind. I set aside some for the furniture and some that would cater for our son's school fee. Our first born was due to start school at the beginning of the following year. I told Charles about my plan for the new furniture; he however advised me that the carpenters would charge me exorbitantly if they did not know the customer. So he offered to take the contract to one of his friends who he said was a "very good" carpenter. I gave Charles the money; he promised that the seats would be ready in a week's time, however, a week turned into weeks and weeks to months, and months to years.

It took five months before I got any feedback on the furniture issue. Charles avoided my questions about the seats. He did this by either coming very late in the evenings or drinking too much and therefore not being in a position to hold any reasonable conversation. We were drifting apart again. We played the cat and rat chase game. Although we lived in the same house, Charles would look for the slightest excuse to be away from me so that I could not ask any questions about the furniture. I did not want to drift to my abusive nature again, so I kept quiet but wondered what happened. Anytime I mentioned about the seats, we would quarrel. I was adamant; I wanted to know if the seats were ready and if so, when were they being delivered by the so called "carpenter friend."

Charles gave a lot of lies when he was willing to talk. One time he left the house telling me that he was going to bring them. Oh, how excited I was. I even told my neighbor, my children and an electrician who had been working on the electrical system around the house. I told them how my house was going to look different just in a few hours' time. I was wrong. That day, Charles did not come home until very late in the evening. When he finally showed up, he was drunk and with that face that tells you, "I am just as disappointed as you are, so please ask no questions." There were no seats.

Another time he told me that the carpenter had traveled to his home in the reserve. Other times he said that the carpenter had not opened his workshop for a whole day for reasons not known to anyone. The list of lies went on and on. I was tormented and tired by all these lies. Charles knew and sensed that I was not happy and knew something was not right. Never at any one time, though did I think that he had used the money for any other thing and that there was no carpenter involved at all. I just kept thinking the carpenter was actually playing tricks on him; I was annoyed with the "imaginary carpenter" and not Charles. That is what love does, it trusteth all things.

So one day I told Charles to take me to the carpenter, I wanted to talk to him personally. He had not expected this from me. He did not want to take me to see this man. He started playing tricks with the idea of the carpenter's place. So he told me to meet him in a particular restaurant; I was so anxious and excited at the same time. I was at the appointed place on time. Charles was however, not there. I sat there waiting for him for about forty five minutes. When he showed up he said abruptly,

"Guess what? Just as I was coming here, I bumped in to the carpenter who was traveling to his home with his family, so we can't go at his place, since nobody is there."

"Ah" I sighed and wondered, what a coincidence? I was terribly hurt but played it down. I was cool.

"When are they coming back?" I asked

"They are going for a week" was his answer.

My mind went running, therefore, they will be back by the following weekend. My mind wondered over the US $1.700 sacrifice that I had saved for this purpose; I wondered whether Charles was genuine or not?

The week past quickly, and we followed the same procedure. He went out first and I had to wait for him at the same restaurant. If you asked me then why we would not go together, I would not have had the answer, because that was my question and I never got any satisfying answer. Anyway, when he came, he said,

"Honey, let's find some place and talk"

"Talk, Why? Are we not going to the carpenter to pick up our furniture?" I asked.

"Please, understand me," he pleaded.

So I gave in to his request. I however, sensed that this was another delaying tactic, only I didn't know what lie he was going to come up with this time around?

We went to the Park, while there he said, "honey, I have to tell you something I have been hiding from you all these time. The carpenter sold the materials I bought to make the seats but he promised he would pay me back."

"What?" I almost jumped out of my skin. I was tongue tied. It felt as though someone had hit me to an unconscious state of mind. It hit me so hard like a thorn piercing through a wound.

What did Charles expect me to say or do in such a situation? My own salary for several years had been moving between US $150 and US $ 500 because of paying his debts. Now I had sacrificed to have my house look better after so many years and this is what I was getting. How did he expect me to trust him in the later years with any finances? To this day, whether he was paid back the money or not, I don't know, or even whether there was a real carpenter or not, only God is the Judge, I do not know. He however confirmed that he had been buying time to tell me this. I wondered then, if that was the truth. There may have been no carpenter; he might have just used that money on the same day I gave it to him for his own purpose, who knows but him and of course God.

The December of 1991 was wonderful. Although there were no new furniture as I had expected and planned. As I had mentioned earlier, that our son was going to start school the following year, I had separated some money for his school fee including his admission fee.

One day Charles said, "You know honey, it is not good to keep money in the house, let me go and bank this money safely in the bank."

It is amazing how Charles found it so easy to just play with my mind set always when it came to finances.

So I agreed and said, "of course"

"That is exactly what I meant, when I said, no one can pull you back but yourself." Carolina rudely interrupted my flow. "At this particular juncture you would have said NO, and you had every right, but you did not." She went on.

I kept quiet because I saw the sense in everything she said. Carolina was very right I had a very recent incident with the furniture that I could have rightfully refused to give Charles any money at all. But, I agreed.

"So he took the money," I continued, "and went to bank it supposedly. When he came back in the evening, I asked him if he banked it."

"Did you bank the fee?"

"Yes, I did." He replied.

"In what bank did you go?" I inquired.

Silence.

"Where is the deposit slip?" I asked again.

Silence.

Then he retorted aloud, "I told you I banked the money, wait and see the day the boy will be going to school, the money will be there, and there will be no problem."

I kept quiet never said a word about it again.

Time passed, and it was time for us to purchase the school uniforms and pay the fee. It was a long story when I asked about the money. Charles gave me an array of excuses. He said, "I decided to do some business with the money so that by the time the boy would be going to school, the amount would have doubled."

What I wondered was that, he usually asked me for money for a different reason, while his heart's intent was another. Why did he lie to me so? Was he afraid his plans were not legal or I would not support him or agree to these plans? I could not answer these questions. What I know is that, at the time I was so naïve and innocent I never read in between the lines of his words. I took him at his word. After all he was my husband and the bible says, in Philippians that we should not think evil but good.

> *"Finally brethren, whatsoever things are true, whatsoever things are honest, whatsoever things are just, whatsoever things are pure, whatsoever things are lovely, whatsoever things are of good report, if there be any virtue , and if there be any praise, think on these things."*
> *(Philippians 4:8)*

However, these continuous episodes would later affect my trust towards him.

Anyway, this pained me so much, more so when it came in hot pursued of the furniture issue. Now I believed that I was being conned like so many others. The only difference was that I was being conned by my own husband. From this day on, I made a promise and swore to myself never again to listen to him in any way concerning money. I realized what a hard heart he had, to manage to hurt my heart without caring a pinch, although he was always sorry for his actions, or was it just that he said so? I am not sure he meant it or it was just from the mouth, while his heart was far from being sorry.

It was too much for me to bear all these. So one time I reported all these episodes to his parents at home. When he was asked what he did with all the money I gave him. And why the businesses never succeeded, he told his parents in my presence, saying,

"You know sincerely speaking; I don't know why I cannot pass a bar whenever I have money on me. I do not know what devil pulls me to these bars to just have a drink?" Charles said oblivious of the impact this revelation was going to have on me.

This was a painful shock to me. I almost fainted and I felt nauseated as though I would throw up. It was mixed with desperate anxiety, looking for answers to why we lived the way we lived. It was more painful also because he was making this confession just a week after I had just buried my father.

It was then that it dawned to me that he used to come with excuses of business plans and ideas so that he could get money from me, knowing quite well inside his heart, that there was no business goal at all. All he wanted was money to drink. Does drinking really take a bulk of money? The kind of money he was asking for? Does one have to have large sums of money to drink? Charles had capitalized on my desperate need to improve our lives and economical status. My sincere need to help him uplift himself and my love for him, he took them all for granted and misused it.

I cannot imagine, he actually brought himself together and asked me for US $ 30,000 just to drink as I was left earning just US$150, while repaying it back for him? And yet I was still the one who had to feed the family and pay the rent while he went out drinking and having a good time, only to come home and lie to me that he had been out all day trying this and that, and had traveled this way or that way? No wonder, he used to be so drunk every day. Oh, how my heart pained to think or even to imagine this. How does one struggle to maintain a family for a man? Is it not our family together? Someone please answer me. Oh God I pray, you see this and answer me. How do I go on? How can I take this and still be able to wake up and have the strength to go on?

I thank the LORD for His word that warns about the love of money being the root of all evil, which while some coveted after, they have erred from faith, and pierced themselves through with many sorrows (1Timothy 6:10). Charles' love of money was causing a lot of sorrows in our lives. There was definitely a lack of faith in God, while his faith was on the bottle my faith was on his ability to somehow, in a magical way get us out of the miserable situation we were in. We both missed the mark. Forgetting what the Word says in John 15:5-6 that "I am the vine, ye are the branches: He that abideth in me, and I in him, the same bringeth forth much fruit: *for without me ye can do nothing…*" We were like two blind men leading each other, and definitely not bearing any fruit in our endeavours. We had forgotten that if the Lord does not build the house, the builder buildeth in vain, as His word says clearly, "Unless the LORD builds the house, its builders labor in vain. Unless the LORD watches over the city, the watchmen stand guard in vain"

But God full of His mercy, through His word that is quick, and powerful and sharper than any two edged sword, piercing even to the dividing asunder of soul and spirit, and of the joints and marrow, and is a discerner of the thoughts and intents of the heart (Hebrews 4:12) was calling us to come "…For we have not an High Priest which cannot be touched with the feeling of our infirmities, but was in all points tempted like as we are, yet without sin. (v.15) and He kept on calling us and urging us through His word "… Let us therefore come boldly unto the throne of grace that we may obtain *mercy*, and find *grace* to help in time of need (v. 16).

I needed this mercy and grace so much. I cried for the mercy and grace of God to cover me because if not, I was not able to make it on my own.

1992

The year 1992 was a difficult one for my family. My father kept on being sick and had to be admitted in various hospitals ranging from nursing homes to major hospitals. He was diabetic and had high blood pressure, these combination made his malaria baits complicated.

One May day, my father had a terrible stroke while in the bathroom. Surprisingly, at this period he had been fine and a happy man. The stroke left his left side paralyzed. He was admitted to the intensive Care Unit at a private hospital. He was in a coma and was hooked on those machines for a week. During this time, our whole family gathered around the hospital. My grandmother had traveled from the reserve and other relatives too. All we saw him do was lay down in bed. At times when I went in I saw him lift his right leg and straightening it again. He just lay there with his eyes open looking at me. I talked to him and I believed he heard me but could not respond. He looked lifeless, but I had hope that he would come back to life. I shared with one sister in Christ at work about my father's condition and she had said, "The devil wants to take your father away."

She was right, my father died on the eighth day. The funeral arrangements were finalized. We had to travel to the reserve for his burial. Among my father's nine children, there were only two of us who had completed school and were working. The rest were still either in school or in college. It was sad; I still do not know how my brother went to break the news to my sister who was away in boarding school. It was sad like all deaths, when they strike in any family. It was after this burial that Charles had confessed what he had been doing all these years.

After all the burial activities were finalized, I traveled back to work in the City. If I had said that the year 1992 was a difficult one, pardon me. God turned things around. When I got to my desk, I had only one mail. It was from the College I had applied to. It had been my dream and prayer to further my education and pursue the library profession. This mail was an answer to my prayer. I had been admitted for a Diploma Course in Library Science. This was good news to me since I had been pursuing a scholarship at the Department of Education, and my being sponsored depended on whether or not I got admission into the College. Therefore, immediately I embarked on pursuing the sponsorship and gladly, it came through successfully.

I joined the prestigious College among other students. All new students were to report on the first of September for a two year Diploma Course. Despite all the joy of admission and the scholarship paying for my tuition, those two years proved to be very challenging since I was still struggling financially. But this felt different. I had hope, I felt happy even in the struggle. I kind of saw a flicker of light from a far in the tunnel's dark part that I was in and I kept moving closer and closer to reach that light.

My struggles went on as usual, with a meager pay, two children to feed, a rent to pay and a jobless husband to take care of. Most of the times, Charles would walk from where we lived, to his sister's house to see if his sister could help us even with one meal. At times he would be successful and get some food or little money to help us get one meal. This begging is just about all he could manage to do genuinely without having to lie. This was not strange anymore. Begging had been the trend of our lives for several years now, since April 1987, it actually never ended until November 1994, when I got a very well paying job, after I graduated.

Again during college holidays like before, I never went back to the office but looked for part time jobs to supplement my earnings. One time I got a secretarial job at a Company situated at a very high class area. I later conferred to the manager who helped me a lot. I asked him if he knew a place I could get a paid internship. I was in hope that he would allow me to do my internship at his organization. I was tired of begging and I needed to do something to stop it immediately if possible. I had had a thorough internship at a major University library and I did not think I needed another vigorous internship. I needed to work and get experience and earn a living. I needed money now. My two children were now going to school and I needed to pay fee for their schooling.

This man was kind and he knew the importance of a profession. He actually referred me to her daughter who worked at a Foundation that needed a librarian to set up a children's library for them.

"Did he say setting up a library?"

I would love that challenge. I had done it once before but not from the scratch. I had been called upon once to help reorganize the World Health Organization's (WHO) Library when they moved to their offices at the Hill Towers. I would definitely like to do it again. This time my interest diverged to the challenge this posed rather than the money.

Therefore, I did my internship at the Foundation.

Initially, I was interviewed by the manager, Agatha. She had asked me to put in writing what I would do for the organization in setting up the library. I did so starting with the fact that I would need to evaluate their interest, the collection and who their intended clientele would be. I would then catalogue, classify and shelve the collection accordingly. I added that I would use an appropriate classification system as per the clientele.

When I presented these ideas and plans to her, she was pleased and took me on immediately. I did all as I had stated and later I held a meeting for all the staff on how to continue running the collection after I had gone back to college. This had appealed to the manager and I had favor with her. She later offered me a job as the Librarian.

AT THE FOUNDATION

The Manager here, as I mentioned earlier, was Agatha. She was actually a foreigner. She treated me kindly and I confided in her about my husband's jobless situation. She was sympathetic and at times could allow me to have advance payments which would be deducted when I was paid my salary. These advance payments helped carry us through to the end of the month.

She extended this kindness further by inviting Charles to help with a few jobs here and there for a little pay. I was delighted. Charles had something to do; although it may sound meager, but this gave him a reason to live; to have somewhere to go in the morning.

When I finally completed my internship period of three months, I was asked to leave my contact in case they needed me for anything. I gave my mother's contact. To my joy, Agatha always called me to help with some work at a fair pay.

In November of 1994, my children had been sent out of school for lack of fee payment. I was preparing for my final examinations, I had no house help, I had not paid my house rent for the month of October and now November was here, things were so bad. I had not managed to get any job this time around. I was desperate. I had no food for the family; I did not know where I was coming from, neither where I was heading to. All of a sudden things were not just moving, everything was at a standstill. What was I to do? Charles was just there, he never went anywhere, and he said he had no place to go. His sister who had helped us all along had somehow indicated, not in words, but in actions that we had become a burden.

Seeing my children at home for just US$ 200 each per semester, which had accumulated to US $ 2000, was painful. I tried selling vegetables from door to door this I had done before, to the nearby affluent neighborhood. As before, I would wake up very early in the morning, left everybody else a sleep. I came back with the vegetables to find them still sleeping. I then tied the vegetables in suitable portions and went through a quarry to the neighboring area which was about three kilometers away. It is this same vegetable that I also divided and left for my family to feed on. I did this every day, never taking a bus but walking to and fro.

I felt hurt everyday whenever I came back and found Charles still asleep, why was he not concerned the way I was? How could he even manage to sleep as though everything was fine, being the man of the house? Why could he not go out just to find something? I was worn out physically, emotionally and mentally since I was also studying in preparation for the final examination, which was due in a month. One evening not able to contain my anger, I challenged him saying that I would not give him food if he could not go and fend for it. How could a man with two children and a wife to take care of just sit and sleep in the house the whole day? I asked him; doesn't the Lord God say in His word that

"He becometh poor that dealeth with a slack hand; but the hand of the diligent maketh rich" (Proverbs 10:4)?

As I went knocking at doors and selling vegetables in that area, I bumped into the houses of some of my former school mates in high school. Some of them had not gone to college, but seemingly doing well, of course others did go to college but had graduated earlier than I. As it turned out these friends are the ones, who helped me with food, bus fare and any other help I needed. I in turn made sure that I passed through their houses to sell them some vegetables, tomatoes and onions and saved them time to go to the market, it worked well. Thank God for His providence.

My friends had been blessed and they were leading better lives than I was. As a human being and in the flesh, I started comparing their lives to mine. I thought to myself, mmhh, and their husbands held good positions in good organizations and were able to take care of things, unlike mine who was waiting for me to fend for him. These thoughts took the better part of me and I started complaining and even threatened to leave Charles. At times he would ask me, "What do you want me to do? Do I steal? I am trying but I cannot get a job, after all, aren't jobs given by God?"

One of my friends Desiree, a former high school friend, was married with two daughters. Her husband was an Engineer, a graduate from one of those prestigious Universities. From the type of the furniture they had, a car and a house to cup it all, one could tell they were doing well. They were a very happy family from how they related to each other. Desiree therefore could give me lots of food from her house and some money for bus fare.

The other friend Joan was a childhood friend, we grew up together. Our parents were both well to do and she was sympathetic, having known my background. Her husband was in the same college as I was. So she was undergoing a difficult time too. So the best we could do was to help one another with whatever small we had. We talked about our difficulties, our hopes, our fears, disappointments and just gave each other encouragement. Her husband graduated before I did and got promoted to a Branch Manager position of the company he had been working for. Joan's woes were over, mine took a different dimension.

The late Judy was the other friend; she had grown up in the reserve. Whenever my family visited grandma, we would spend time together. Her family had been wealthy too, so she was also sympathetic at what I was going through having known my background. Judy had graduated and was doing well. Her husband was doing very well too. He had a motor vehicle business and was buying and selling all kinds of models. They drove very good cars and exchanged them just as one would clothes. She also helped me quite a lot. Despite her college education, she was not working; they had decided for her to stay at home, her size had tripled from the slim lady I had known as a teenager.

Comparing my life to these friends took a toll on me. One night I remember being filled with anguish and agony. I could not sleep; I just cried out to God and poured my heart out to Him. I quoted all the scriptures I could remember, asking Him where I had gone wrong? I had gotten saved in the fifth grade, and had tried to live a Christian life. Why was my life such a misery? I reminded God that his word said that we come and reason together, (Isaiah 1:18a) I asked God if my children would ever go to school? I remember my spirit actually praying for my mother in-law and everybody else. I remembered how in the Bible Hannah, Prophet Samuel's mother had cried to God to bless her with a child. She was agonized with Peninah's attitude towards her barrenness. I cried some more praying for a miracle because I could not go on this way. My heart was literally aching on this night. I was in pain over school fees for my children, over the house rent and just my general situation. I was tormented by the fact that on some nights we had no lights at all and were forced to open the door at night, to use the moonlight; at such times, I just used to leave the door wide open as I prepared our meals, or as we waited for Charles to come back, praying that he had succeeded to get a meal for the family. One thing I remember is that at such times of waiting, the children and I used to sing and pray. Our songs were mainly songs of praise to the Almighty, and true to His word, He would always provide an answer. Charles would come home with something. We literally lived from hand to mouth, one hour at a time. One hour I would be seriously studying for my upcoming examinations without knowing what the family would eat, and the next hour I would be out there looking for something from my neighbors, or friends in the nearby area. We would look for lunch, then immediately after lunch we would take off to go look for supper.

What God gave me at this time was favor with my friends. Sabrina was yet another friend from my work place. She was a tall and slender lady. We had shared the same office before going to college. She had taken Business Administration. She was still single and had a good job after graduating. She had known me before all these problems started and was taken aback at how things had turned out. She confided to me that my situation made her fear marriage. Anyway she was also very kind to me and could give me bits of money for food and bus fare. There was a time she even took me to her house and gave me some descent nice clothes because I had not bought new ones for a long time. I think it must have shown whenever I went to visit her in her office. She might have felt embarrassed; she offered to give me a whole wardrobe of her former clothes. I was delighted because the idea of clothes had not even crossed my wildest dreams. I was focused on feeding not clothing.

My day normally ended quite late than other people. Once I came from school, I had to pass through a friend or two to get some food and bus fare for the next day every day before going to the house. For this reason, I usually reached home very late in the evening. Sometimes I would walk from these friends' houses as I budgeted on what I had, reaching home as late as 8:00pm. This was the time we would start cooking what I had just brought for dinner.

One particular night, of course like many other times before, I felt this life was so overwhelming. I couldn't take it no more. I thought about the word of God and the story of Job, how he went through the testing period. I cried to God and asked Him many questions. "Why?" I wondered, "Had it been me? I had been a studious girl in school. The worst grade I ever brought home during my secondary school education had been a "B." That was considered a second position among over 40 students. Where did I go wrong? What bothered me most was my children, would they ever go to school? What about my husband, was he ever going to be anybody in life? I would always pray for Charles so much, I never prayed for myself. As I sit writing this, we have been ten years in this marriage and he has been nine years and five months without a job. Anytime God answered my prayer and gave him a good job, he never stayed on it. He had this bad habit of swindling money from the companies.

So, on this particular night, I felt so helpless, and I cried out to God. I cried my heart out and a usual reasoned with Him. "If you are my father," I said, "God don't you think I am already too tired of all these, for how long am I to go on like this, was it not enough?" I prayed so long till the wee hours of the morning. After this prayer, I felt a peace over me. A peace that I had never felt before, I felt almost as though a burden had been removed from off my shoulder. I had told my Father in Heaven everything I could not share with anybody. I repented all the sins I knew and those I did not know. I felt happy and went to sleep very peaceful. All of a sudden I had a conviction and a witness within my heart that He had heard me. I knew deep within my heart that He had heard me and was going to do something, just what, I did not know but I felt an assurance in the peace, so I slept soundly.

In the morning, I woke up and was ready to get out of the door to go to college. Suddenly there was a knock at the door, it was my younger brother. He had a message for me. Agatha the manager where I had done my internship and set up the children's library had contacted my mother and wanted to see me immediately.

Oh, no! I really wanted to revise for my final examinations; I did not really want to work for money now. God would know how to feed us. Anyway, I went to see Agatha. She was in her office as usual busy at her papers. When I entered and after the formal greetings she said,

"Dianne, I have not called you to work now, I know that whenever I call you, you see the US$ 400. I am calling you for something different"

Before I had time to wonder through my mind what could be different, Agatha went on

"I am offering you a position here. You have potential, I have seen it. I am not sure but I have prayed about it and I think I have the answer. I have talked it through with the Board of Directors, and they are in agreement."

I stood there in awe, I knew God had given me peace and I had a conviction last night when I prayed that He was surely going to do something... but...but... did He move this fast, I had slept last night around 4:00am in the morning, my brother had come just about 7:00 am as I was just about to leave for school. I was in Agatha's office at 9:00am. Did God move that fast to answer prayers? I realized that in the spiritual realm there is no time and there is no distance. His Holy Spirit had moved.

Agatha invaded my train of thought,

"You can come in as an Administrative Assistant since we have none at the moment, and meanwhile, since we intend to run a fully fledged children's library, you will be developing it and then move in to your position as the Librarian for the organization."

God had answered my prayers immediately. My cry of the previous night had reached Him. While I was praying Agatha too had been praying. And God woke her up, she confessed to me and said she did not know why but she could not sleep the previous night. The Lord had disturbed her peace and she could not be at peace until she had obeyed the LORD and told me what the Lord wanted me to have for my answer. The Lord got her mind working, and she did not want to wait another day, she had to see me this morning. Praise be to God. Oh how merciful is our God, how Faithful is He. And His goodness and Mercy endureth forever. All my life till then, I had lived by His grace. I would probably be divorced, dead through suicide, because all these had gone through my mind not once. But God, my only Father, who owns the universe kept me safe from all these. Now it was time for Him to turn things around for me. It was time for my double portion. He had just begun. He had given me a job in a private sector. I did not apply for the job, I did not do the interview, and all I did was prayed to my Father God.

Well, I did not know what to say at this good news. I promised Agatha that I would contact my mother and husband for their opinion. She understood and was willing to wait. So she said, "Yes, of course, I will give you time to be sure and when you make up your mind and have peace with the offer, just call me."

When I asked how much she would pay me, she never gave me a figure but said, "not much but I am sure it is far much better than what they are giving you at the Department of Health."

It was not difficult to make up my mind. I went straight to class and told my friend Sally. She scolded me saying I was "crazy" to even ask for time to consider the offer. She added, "That is a life time opportunity, take it." My mom was worried about job security considering that she was also a government employee, but she was agreeable. Charles was just grateful. So the next day I was at Agatha's office to confirm my acceptance to the offer. I got the job, but I was to start later after my final examinations were over.

As I was coming out of Agatha's office, I went into the general office to say hello to the other staff members. The Accountant was happy to see me and immediately gave me a number to call. She said she had wanted to call me because I was in her mind when she heard that the Administrator to the Chairman needed a librarian on a part time basis to help organize the collection they had. She urged me to please call Christine, for that was the Administrator's name. I called Christine immediately and we set an appointment for the following day. I got the job. It was on a part time basis so I did it over the weekends.

Praise be to God, are you seeing God at work here? The truth is God gave me two jobs on the night I was crying to Him; one full time and one on a part time basis. Isn't God great? Yes, He is. He had just turned my mourning in to dancing. My heart was full of joy. I felt like Job when God turned the captivity of Job when he prayed for his friends; also God gave him twice as much as he had before (Job 42:1).

SCHOLARSHIP

Sitting down at my desk in a class of about thirty students; each one of us in their own world, unable to communicate. My eyes roamed around the room. I noticed that the desks were small compared to the ones I knew back at home. The blackboard was movable, wow! And there were no chalks. Hanging over the blackboard was a screen. There was a computer attached to the teacher's table. No wonder we were called third world, Africa lags behind in technology.

All the students came from different parts of the world; some Japanese, Chinese, Eastern European, and Africa. The only thing we all had in common was our need to learn the German language. We listened attentively to the teacher as she let out the words with ease "Guten Abend". This was my first day of my Deutsche Sprach Kurse. She added, "ich heisse Frau …." And let out a name. In my mind I thought, she must be introducing herself to us.

As she went on teaching, I thought that words in the German language were very long. However, when she wrote the words on the board, it seemed that the words were written exactly as they were pronounced. One evening she said something that caught my attention. We were learning about nouns, so that we would be able to introduce ourselves. She said, "die Armbanduhr" meaning "a watch." This was very descriptive to me. Later on I came to see it clearly, this was a noun composed of three nouns, which made it a little longer than the length of the word "watch." The descriptive nature of the language struck me. "die Armbanduhr" is worn around the arm, it has a band and it tells the hour. I loved the discovery.

Alphabets were a challenge. Letter "W" was pronounced as "V" and "V" was pronounced as "Fao" "J" was pronounced as "yot" and "Y" as "Yipsilon". The alphabets were pronounced the way we would say the vowels "a e i o u" only with an accent. They had extra letters for double "ss, "a" and "o" either using a symbol or adding something they called an "umlaut."

As I kept attending the German language class, I wondered; How was I going to be able to learn the alphabets and sing them the way I sang my a,b,c,d…as a child? Would I pronounce them correctly? Some words like "Ich" had a "kh" sound, would I be able to say them? I made a decision that I was going to make it. I decided to borrow tapes from the library. I listened intently and closely to the pronunciations. As I listened I opened my mouth wide, twisting my lips and letting the words come out of my mouth, repeating what I heard from the tapes. I "devoured" those tapes repeating the words over and over as though my whole life depended on them. For the alphabets, I even invented my own phonetics; sometimes using words in my own mother tongue to help me remember the sound of each letter of the alphabet.

As I struggled with the alphabets and the pronunciations, something else was in store for me. If I thought that the alphabets were a challenge, there was a bigger one in store, that I have not been able to fully master to this present day. In German language, every noun has its own gender and therefore a different article. Now, for those of us, who are French or Spanish speakers or other languages with a gender to each noun, it would be normal; to me, this was "Greek." You see, I spoke Swahili, Luo and English, and none of these three had such grammatical rules. The only articles in the English language are "the", "a" and "an." A noun is just a noun. A noun cannot be a male, a female or a neutral. Here I was being taught that:

A watch is a feminine noun hence the article "die Uhr"

A baby was neutral hence "das Baby"

A table was masculine hence "der Tisch"

How was I to master the gender of all the nouns in this new grammatical rule? I found out that there was no general rule. Sometimes a rule would apply to some nouns but not all. For instance, I found out that nouns ending with "e" or "ung" tended to be feminine. However, there were other feminine nouns that didn't follow this rule. So I decide to learn the gender as I learnt the nouns.

This whole issue of "der, die, das" and the male, neutrality and femininity of nouns was not my cup of tea. My head was spinning; this was too much for me; to add salt to injury, every noun, had to begin with a capital letter. This was not an easy class. I didn't understand it. For example, "a cup" is "die Tasse." I remember thinking, that is not right but no! That is called "die Rechtschreibung" meaning "the correct grammar." How on earth did I end up here? I asked myself one day when it seemed too much.

Well it all started with a phone call from Agatha, our manager. Her voice had carried an unusual excitement. She had important news to share with me before it was brought to the attention of the other staff members. I had been working at the Foundation for six months after graduating and from the day God answered my prayers.

According to Agatha, it happened that in one of her meetings with the then Germany's Cultural Attaché, they had offered a three months scholarship to the librarian of our organization, and that was me.

God had turned things around and for my shame I was having double and for my confusion all these years, I was rejoicing in my portion, therefore, in my land I was possessing the double: everlasting joy was unto me. (Isaiah 61:7). I was greatly rejoicing in the LORD, my soul was and is still joyful in my God; for He hath clothed me with the garments of salvation, he hath covered me with the robe of righteousness, as a bridegroom decketh himself with ornaments, and as a bride adorneth herself with her jewels (v.10).

For as the earth bringeth forth her bud, and as the garden causeth the things that are sown in it to spring forth; so the Lord GOD was causing righteousness and praise to spring forth before all the nations, for His glory (v.11)

All I could do was listen to Agatha in awe at the mighty Hand of God upon my life.

At our meeting, Agatha did not give me an option to think. This was for the organization; it would open doors of opportunities for me and for the organization. It was for a mutual benefit…she went on excitedly. In my mind I kept on asking myself, God but why Germany? Of all the places I had dreamt of, the U.K and the U.S.A had been on the top of the list since I already spoke the English language, but Germany, never thought of it.

As I landed at the Frankfurt Flughafen, I felt lost. It was my first time ever to travel abroad, thank God for one of my friends, a German language teacher at the Goethe Institute, who had changed her travel plan to attend a German language refresher course, to travel with me. At my final destination, SchIoss Blutenburg in Munich, I was met by Frau Iris, a slim tall German lady who introduced me to Dr. Carmen, a short, plumb Italian lady. She was also here for the same Stipendium program. Later I met Maria an elderly professor from the University of Tel Aviv; there were two other male professors from Montreal, Canada and Lithuania (one of the former Soviet Union States), and one more female professor from the University of Bulgaria. Although we were all here to carry out research in various fields of knowledge, one could tell that we had a language barrier, however, we all spoke some English.

As time went by, I knew I needed the German language, and that is how I ended up in this class. The classes started in early September. The weather was still warm and pleasant. The class was at 5:00 pm. As time went by all of a sudden, the leaves on the trees begun to fall and loosing color. As the daytime saving came in, I remember coming out of the library one afternoon to go to my class and it was dark. I looked at my watch; it said 5:00 pm. I thought to myself, something must be wrong. It was only later that I learnt about day time saving. See, I came from Africa right at the equator, and the length of night and that of the day are equal all the year round. So I had no idea what awaited me.

Well, I had known something about multi-tasking, but this one, I was not prepared for. It started getting chilly, cold and windy; with yellow and red leaves everywhere. When I came to work in the morning, it was dark and when I left to go back to my room in the afternoon, it was dark. It was dark all the time. I could not take the whole stress and anxiety of my research which was now due in a month, and a report of my trip, meetings with prospective donors and all the activities that were part of the package of the scholarship program ...I dropped the language class.

As I went back home to my country, I realized that this class had awakened a yearning desire in me to learn the

German language; a desire that I had to satisfy. I thank God that I had the opportunity to do so, as I chose to go back to Germany and lived there for eleven years. Only then, "did the coin drop" and with an open mind and the little background I had gained, I started to read and write the German language. It became my fourth language. With this knowledge, I managed to be a translator, an English teacher to IBM Company in Schweinfurt, Germany and it has empowered me and made me who I am today. I noted that one can only learn a language when one resides in the land in which that language is spoken.

My scholarship was for a Fellowship program, at the International Youth Library in Munich, Germany. It was for a period of three months from the beginning of September to end of November, 1995. While there, I was able to complete my research paper entitled "Folktale: a source of scientific knowledge to children."

The completion of the paper and even from its initial conception was made possible by all those around me and those I worked for. To whom I am grateful. Agatha, the manager, the Chairman of the Organization and the staff at the Internationale Jugendbibliothek (IJB) were all very cooperative. The presence of an up to date and efficient information tools was encouraging. Tools such as catalogues, professional journals were up to date. Information and documentation services were efficient, my questions were answered satisfactorily. The books I needed were promptly brought to my desk. The staff was quite friendly.

Planned tours and cultural visits to the ancient Castles of King Ludwig II, visits to the Opera performances and classical orchestras performing Beethoven and Mozart were all part of the scholarship packages all these introduced me to the European Culture and lifestyle and gave me a real taste of European traditions. I received a Diplomat treatment in everything, rubbing shoulders with Diplomats and High ranking officials and professionals. I gave interviews and speeches. I had a stipend allowance of DM 1,500 per month. God had really turned my mourning into dancing. It felt wonderful.

In my work, I looked critically at folktales from various parts of the world with a view of finding out if they carried any scientific element. I then used them to illustrate my point. For every folktale, I made an analysis and an authoritative evaluation of the following:

1. Attention to the scientific and technological information it contained.

2. Appropriateness of the illustrations to the intended age group.

3. Coordination of the text and the illustrations.

4. Appropriateness of the tale to the intended audience by age.

Dr. Barbara Scharioth, the Director of the IJB felt it was a good idea to show the children the worthwhile technical processes and scientific elements through a story because children respond more easily to this indirect approach than the direct manner found in text books. She believed with good books for the children, this could be very effective.

I found out that German's had used various approaches to impart scientific knowledge to children. During an interview with Dr. Andrea Bode, the Chief Librarian of the IJB, he said, the Germans' scientific and technological achievement had developed approximately 200 years of the 2nd half of the 18th Century through to the 19th Century. During this time, the pedagogues had to find new ways of teaching the children techniques that exist today. They had to find new ways of writing children's books with scientific information passed along in a story form. They made sure that the books were pleasurable, easy to read but gave the history and principles of the techniques they contained.

He went on to say, that these books were meant to teach the children the techniques of how they could be masters of handling science and technology rather than be governed by it. In this manner, the pedagogues wrote books on civilization, technology, environmental control etc. The books, he said, usually contained interesting fictional stories with illustrations on various scientific subject areas.

I was happy that I was not far from the truth. A folktale is a tale that one just evokes into existence by piercing together things out of common experience. What I intended to say in this research paper, was that in passing a scientific knowledge through a folktale, we already know the concept we want to pass on to the children. It is therefore our task to find a mode of transmitting this concept, and we choose the folktale as the means or the mode of transmission; this makes the concept, more interesting, motivating and memorable, and of course carries our lesson.

While there, I also managed to make professional contact with Leoba Batten, the Director of Books for All, a project affiliated with UNESCO, Helene Schar of Baobab in Switzerland, Haike Brandt of Stiftung Organization in Berlin, and Barbara Geldberg of Belitz and Gelberg. I also managed to visit various professional and social events and institutions, such as the State Library in Munich and the children's sick room library of the Children's Cancer Center. I attended various cultural events like the Munich October Fest, and generally had a great time as I worked.

JANUARY 1997

I had been in this organization for three years now. I had worked hard, professionally. I thought I could try and spread my wings elsewhere; the grass is always greener on the other side of the river. It was a warm day on this 29th day of January. I was at my desk in my office but my mind was not at work. I wanted so much to get another well paying job. I had heard of several upcoming opportunities in some International schools, I thought I had to find a way of getting out of the office to get to one of these prospective employers. My mind went round and round looking for a convincing, genuine excuse to get permission.

In actual sense, one would wonder why I was even thinking of another job, while I had a great one. However, the reality was that, the job was satisfying and challenging, which I liked, but the salary was stagnant. Since I joined the organization three years ago, in spite of all I had done, I had no single increment. My lifestyle had changed a great deal and the expenditure was not proportionate to the income anymore. I marketed the readership program both locally and internationally. I managed to get fund donations towards the program. I felt I had turned an Idea into a reality and we now had a flourishing children's library, which was at the time, the only one of its kind in the Country and I bet in Africa – a unique children's library. Nothing was ever done to increase even a single penny to my pay. On the other hand the country's economic status was not stagnant as my salary. The rents were high, school fees went on increasing, bus fares were rocket high and so I was anxious. I also believed that with all my credentials I would be a viable candidate.

My colleagues at the office were friendly and accommodating. Bianca the secretary was a plumpish lady who kept the office alive with her stories. She always had something to say and was very warm. She was also very efficient at her speed typing. Beatrice the accountant was on the other hand a young lady still having all the vigor of life. We were about the same age. Baron, the editor a very quiet young man in his early 30's, had also recently won a scholarship to Boston University. Francis, the office assistant was just as welcoming and warm to all of us; he was a father to everyone. The manager was just as cooperative as much as all of us; she had made us this way. It was a friendly warm caring atmosphere that we worked in. One felt like being in a family. We were also very competent in our own fields of specialization. We worked hard and were loyal, we placed the organization on the top priority. Many people wanted to be part of us. We portrayed prosperity and comfort.

Anyway, I was looking for a job, and therefore determined to get permission to be away from the office. So on this particular day I announced that after lunch I would be going to the bank and also intended to pass through the treasury building where I had some official errands to take care of. That gave the indication that I would be coming late from lunch.

Of course I went to these places too but my main mission was to go to this particular International School. I did not exactly know where it was. One of my friends had given me a vague idea of its location. So I boarded a bus and got off at the Mall. I stood there for a while looking for someone I could trust well enough to ask where the school was. I saw this young lady apparently in her late teen age. She was plumb, with a dark complexion. She had a nice hair do.

"Excuse me please?" I said almost shouting because of the distant between us.

"Yes"

"How do I get to the International School around here, please?"

"The school?" she shouted across to me as she walked towards me. "Just cross the road, then go straight for about one kilometer. You will then see the sign posted there on the road, then eh... or I can take you there since I am going that direction" she said.

"Oh that would be very kind of you" I thanked her.

She had a very fluent English accent. I could not tell from what ethnicity she came from. I am talking of ethnicity here because, during this time, there had been a lot of ethnic groups fighting against each other, burning down houses in the name of ethnic cleansing. So suddenly, people had become conscious of tribal affiliation more than any other time. To me tribe had not mattered previously at all. I had mixed well with people of all backgrounds in my school days and even now. I attended schools in the areas dominated by various tribes, and of course the Capital where I had lived all these years was a cosmopolitan city. However, at this time it was hard to avoid thinking on tribal lines.

As we went a long I realized that my new companion did not know that I was in a hurry to get back to the office, therefore, the pace at which we were walking did not excite me. So I excused myself and got ahead of her. Following her directions I continued straight on until I saw the sign post as she had indicated. This meant that I had to leave the main road and branch off to the left into a dirt road. It took me another one kilometer from the sign post to the school's gate.

The road to the school was a lonely road with a few buildings, to be specific, three large ones on the left hand side, and that was it. There were swampy vegetation but the swamp had dried up in the present drought. On the right, were tall grass, and apart from the occasional one or two cars heading towards the school and a handful construction workers on the roadside, there was no much life to be seen.

The school was located in an upper class Suburb. It was an International school and well built with students from the upper class level. At the gate, I did not find anybody, so I entered in to the compound. As I took a few steps inside the compound I realized how quiet the place was. I could see the students playing in the field, which was far from the entrance and the noise did not even reach anywhere to interrupt the quiet, almost serene atmosphere in the compound.

After a few meters walk, I met the security man who asked me who I wanted to see.

"The Director's Administrative Assistant." I said.

"For a job?" he asked.

"Yes" I decided not to hide my purpose of visit; after all, I was not desperate. I guess sometimes I do this depending on the reception I am given at different places. This man was different; he did not look like a man who was exercising his power in an abusive way. He was genuinely doing his job and directing visitors appropriately. He was tall, slim, wearing a neat navy blue suit and a white shirt, which I thought was the uniform. It was easy to detect from his accent that he was from the same ethnic background as I was. He was quick to ask me my name, in order to fill out the gate pass.

"And what's your name?"

"Dianne A..." I deliberately used my sir name (which I never used) because my official name would not have made it obvious where I came from, but my Sir name said I am from the same tribe as you are.

"You want to be a teacher here?" he asked.

"No, a librarian" I answered.

"Oh Yes, they have a library but I have not seen any staff there yet, try your luck."

He gave me a gate pass to the Director's office, holding it to me he said,

"With the kind of man you are going to see, if you are not of his ethnicity, there is no high probability that you will get the job, he works along tribal lines."

When I look back now, and consider the qualifications I had against my friend who got the job and is now the librarian I agree with him. The only qualification I didn't have was that I was not of the right tribe.

The reception to the Director's office was on the left wing of the Administration block on the first floor. The receptionist was friendly. She was plumb and in her late twenties. She told me to wait as the Director was on the phone and had to clear something with one staff member, then I would go in.

Sitting there for a while gave me time and helped me make my own observation and opinion of the whole situation. Most of the non-teaching staff, (i.e. the secretary, receptionist and a lady at the computer) were all from one ethnic group. The ladies were elegant and at ease in their work. They seemed very much confident in their capacity as staff members. After some time the teaching staff and some students started coming to the staff room since classes were over. I saw that the school catered for white students and the children of the elite.

Two factors, ethnic background and socio-economic status dampened my spirit. Therefore, although I had come with a high determination and confidence to convince the Director whoever he was, that I was the best candidate for the job, I realized now that educational qualifications and a wealth of experience never mattered sometimes. So when my turn came to see the Director and he sharply asked me what I wanted and what my name was, and immediately sent me back to the receptionist to be given the school's address, I was not surprised. He was least interested in me, probably after telling by my name that I was not of his tribe.

Ethnicity had been promoted by the multiparty politics that had just caught up, just like what was happening in various parts of Africa, what with the Rwanda's Tutsis against the Hutus. Ours had not reached that dimension though. Back at the gate, the security man was not surprised. He however advised me to see the Personnel Manager of the school, who he was sure, would not be biased.

That day, I could not go back to the office. So after calling the office, I boarded a bus and headed home. I reached home very early at around 6:00 pm. Charles had not come back; he had money nowadays and probably had passed through a bar to have "one for the road" before coming home.

When he came back that evening, he told me about his sister, (she is deceased now). According to him, the relationship between her and the husband was headed for a divorce. His brother in-law had apparently met an old girlfriend, who claimed that her twenty year old son had been his. This was sad because this had been a marriage of over fifteen years. It was a beautiful family and I felt sorry that this "new-old" girlfriend was going to destroy this wonderful family.

This story did not just come without its implications. Charles straight away started relating her sister's situation to ours. He claimed that I had a boyfriend and that this would lead to our divorce in future.

What I asked him was why he had not claimed that I had a boyfriend before? I would have left him long time when he lost his job in 1987 when we were just newly married. There was not a baby to hold me back then. I reminded him how it had been so rough for me to sustain the family, paying rent, schools fees, clothing, house helper's salary and any traveling expenses both within the city and whenever we visited the village. I reminded him how that in all the nine years we had been together, all I did in whatever circumstance had been geared towards the betterment of our children's lives and their education and they were both in a private school, which I was paying for. I asked him why he had not claimed that I had a boyfriend when he had convinced me to take heavy loans for him, which had left me with as little as US $ 150 as the net pay not for one or two years but for ten years? Why didn't he ever ask in those days how I was managing to pay the rent, bring food home, and have bus fare? Why didn't he ever talk of me having a boyfriend then? I had all the reasons to, if I wanted to. I wondered if he wanted us to go step by step through the painful and hardship period of the past. Why, was he short sighted and only started relating her sister's situation to ours instead of tackling ours separately? Why was he bringing chaos now that I could manage well with no strain?

I said, "Charles, remember that today I can come home straight from work without having to branch somewhere looking for help. Those past years, whenever it was five o'clock and everybody left their offices and school to go home, that is when I started looking for bus fare to take me back to the house and bring me back the next morning to be in place at my work or in school, as the case was. I reminded him how, that was also the time I started looking for food to bring home to the family, always thinking of how to divide it between that evening and the following day for lunch for those who would remain in the house. I reminded him of how I could come home as late as 8:30 pm and find them hungry, waiting for me, while on the other hand I also never knew where the meal was going to come from,"

I said, "Then you had every reason to think I had an extra marital affair, but you didn't, why now?"

I think human beings are never satisfied and tend to look for trouble when there is none. What was bringing this argument did not concern us at all. I thought, sometimes we cry out to God to give us something, and when He does, we forget to thank Him and start brooding over imagined things, and when you brood over things they actually get hatched.

Charles had been blessed with a temporary position at the same organization I worked for. Although we never really worked in the same department, (he was in the Marketing Department and I was in the Readership Development program), we always left for home together.

There was this particular day right after the incident of his sister; we were walking down town with Francis, Charles and I. We conversed as we walked; we talked about many things including the prices of cars, because we had been contemplating buying one. After we departed our ways with Francis, Charles and I still chatted along, it was a nice walk to the bus stop.

Suddenly we bumped into one of the rent-to-own workers where Charles had previously ordered some item from and never paid. He stopped me saying I had not completed paying what my husband owed them, Charles used to put my name as the next of kin, so that way if he could not pay, they turned to the next of kin. This officer had known my previous work place three years before but never knew where I worked for after I left. So he wanted to know where my present work place was in order for them to start taking the deductions again; I thought to myself "No way", I was not going to let Charles' dirty past get me again. I had come a long way, so I did not tell him where I worked. Charles on the other hand never knew this man; they changed their staff and each time a different person dealt with different accounts.

When next I caught up with Charles, he was annoyed and did not want to talk to me. He walked ahead of me as though I was his tail. (If there is one thing I dislike, it is a man walking ahead of me and claiming we are together, I think it is rude). So I decided not to play the catch up game. I totally decided to ignore him, knowing we will meet in the house anyway. I was on my own, thank God for the wide roads, I crossed over the opposite side and mingled with the crowd and headed for the bus stop.

On reaching home, I noticed that he still wanted to sulk. I actually didn't know why he was sulking. So, I let him go ahead as I bought some bananas for the children. I never made to hurry in order to catch up with him. I never had that kind of energy. So I just walked slowly and entered the house after him. His attitude had been changing so abruptly like this whenever he saw me talking to any man.

What I guessed was going on through his mind was that, the man I had stopped to talk to was my boyfriend. He was so depressed that evening, he couldn't sleep, so he went out and came back late.

One Sunday, during the Easter holidays, one of my brothers John came to visit us. He was a very jolly young man who always showed us a few tricks now and then. This day he decided to show us a few tricks on cards. So I asked Charles if he knew where the cards were. He told me to look through some paper bags in our bedroom. When I started looking, the first paper bag that I held and looked through gave me a shock of my life. Charles had tore up two books a friend of mine had sent from Germany. What took me by surprise was that these were novels by African novelists, they were literature materials. They could have been purchased by anyone from any bookstore. They were not personal letters to me, they were published literature.

One of these books was a biography of Buchi Emecheta, an African writer, who I had met when I was in Germany. She had given a lecture on her books and I had admired her. I bought her books and was happy to get her autograph. She had an inner strength that made her stand with her "head above waters" (the title of one of the books) no matter what she went through. This particular book was an inspiration for me to start writing and I had promised myself that I would always use it both as a reference and an inspiration book, since I intended to become a writer. Of course, at the time, I did not have the vaguest idea of what I wanted to write about and so, like Buchi, I decided to keep a diary as a store for my ideas and any information I might need in the future.

Now on this particular moment, what beat me was the fact that I could not understand why he destroyed the books, they had nothing but information. Was this the way a man expressed his love or anger towards a woman? To me this meant two libraries destroyed. But, what was he scared of? Was he fighting to win back my love? Is it not true that one can never force love; and was not love gentle? And all other virtues that I had so often associated with love according to the word of God? Why had he kept on hurting me all these years? Was he scared of loosing me because of what he had done to me in the years? This episode to me was the same with Buchi Emechta's experience when she wrote that her first manuscript was burned by her husband. Of course this was not my manuscript but the impact of it was traumatizing. I asked myself, what had gone so wrong that destroying those books was the only way to vent whatever anger he had against me. Where did he throw his education and ability to discuss issues? Why did he do it secretly? What was in his mind during that process? They were not small books and he must have taken quite a moment to tear them. I had no answers to these questions.

I was totally dumb founded. I never talked again for the rest of that evening apart from asking him why he did it. He had no better answer apart from laughing while asking in my language "does it hurt you so much that I tore them up?" I was tongue tied. What an evil, sarcastic tone. Did he expect me to answer his question? Later in the night, I woke up to put everything down in my diary while he slept. Charles accepts that he is jealous, uncertain of himself and unstable emotionally. According to him I am the one who is able to take care of the family's emotional balance; but I wonder who is to take care of mine?

CHARLES AT WORK

The phone rang and I picked it up. "Hello" I said. This Saturday afternoon I had some work to catch up on, so I was working at our chairman's office.

"Hello" the voice on the other end responded. Immediately, I recognized Agatha's voice.

"Oh, I was wondering if you were at the office, I had something I wanted us to discuss, can we meet somewhere?"

"Yes, of course, no problem, where do you want us to meet?" I asked.

"I hope I am not taking you off your work." She hesitated.

Agatha was always concerned about interference with one's work. When at last we met at our office, she cleared her desk and asked me to join her on her way out. We ended up in her house right in her bedroom. It was not my first time in her house, I had even slept there in more than one occasion whenever we worked late, but in her bedroom, it was my first time ever.

"I want to be the first one to tell you this; I do not want you to hear it from another source." She said.

Agatha had been once again kind enough to take Charles on a temporary appointment to market the organization's magazine. However, according to her he had not brought in US $ 18,700 collected from one client. She had given him time and was at this point devastated. I could very well relate to her frustration, having had such experiences before with Charles.

I was devastated myself and I did not know how to react. Charles should have known that such things could take him to court. I was too hurt. I decided my marriage had come to an end. I felt I could not take any more of these things; they were too much to bear. I did not even have a heart to tell anybody, not even my mother or his parents. Agatha, however, not knowing all what I had been through in this marriage encouraged me to stay on and give him yet another chance. Back at home, when I asked him what had happened, his response was, "were you not told everything by whoever told you?" I was frustrated, why was he so cruel and heartless, in fact unreasonable could be the right word? I asked God what had become of him, I don't understand much about men's brain and emotional changes, but I was sure he needed some counseling.

MAY BOOK EXHIBITION

In my day to day interactions, I have come to realize a few traits that I posses. These would describe my character as a person. I was not born with these traits, but I have acquired them in the years, some through life's experience; some by affiliation and yet some have been influenced by particular events. They have made me a more considerate person who thinks not only of her own self interest but that of others too. They have made me who I am today, following my life's experience.

I have become very protective and caring over my children, I am loyal to friendship and close relations, realizing that during my hard times my friends helped me a lot. I am also flexible and courageous in all my under takings, I however remain focused to my vision in all I do. And most of all I am a very strong believer in the power of God and how He can turn things around for good for those who trust in Him.

Were these my characteristics before? No, Life itself has had some positive impact on the way I think, process my ideas and how I present them. I am more refined and more appreciative of diversity than I was before. My relationship with God has also led to my maturity.

However, I remember one particular incident that helped shape my character to what it is today. I had been working at the organization for about three years. We were the coordinators of the Pan-African Children Book Fair, an annual event held in the last week of the month of May. This event brought together Publishers from all over Africa, who usually held their annual African Publishers Network (APNET) meetings within the Book Fair. It also brought together the regional publishers like the Kenya Publisher Associations - (KPA) in a forum that enabled them discuss issues pertaining to publishing. The event became so popular that on its fifteenth anniversary it had attracted many international donor agencies, writers and illustrators, editors, translators, librarians, and generally everybody in the book world. One such visitor was Mr. Peter Weidhaas, the Director of Frankfurt Book Fair (Frankfurt Buchmesse).

Book Fair preparations and all the events involved used to just zap up everyone's energy. All the coordination and purchases, making sure that everything concerning one's own program ran smoothly. I was the head of Readership Development Program which had to coordinate all seminars and workshops with regards to inculcating the love of reading at an early age. In this I had to locate speakers in their specialized fields of knowledge, and coordinate with them on different topics that would be of interest and relevance to the theme of the Book Fair, which was changed every year. There was the issue of advertisements of the event itself and the various seminars and workshops within the BIG event which was overwhelming. Contingencies such as banners, which were made by a different company and one, had to be there physically in place to follow up. Then we had to get the permission from the City's Authorities for the display of the banners on strategic points of entrance to the city. There was the marketing of the events which included both live and recorded interviews in all media such as radio, television and newspapers. In addition, Agatha made sure that we had video clips made for specific seminars and workshops held both locally and regionally.

On one particular year, I remember feeling very sick and asked to go to the doctor, my supervisor's response was, "Dianne, this is not the time to get sick." The actual Book Fair took a period of five days, although the preparations took six months. Well on the last day of the event, and after I had made sure everybody had dined and danced to cup it all, I was taken ill at midnight and was rushed to the hospital where I stayed for 15 days. I was diagnosed with pneumonia; I thought that was the end of me.

One particular evening as I was lying in my hospital bed, I actually felt that I was slipping into the hands of the spirit of death, I stopped feeling pain and felt like a deep sleep was stealing me away. Suddenly, I remembered my children, in a glimpse I saw what their life under Charles' care would look like, it scared me out of death and I heard myself shouting out loud "No!!!!!" Only at this point did I become aware of my surrounding, I heard the nurses run into my room. I was transferred to another hospital and rushed to the emergency room where they called a chest specialist for me. Within a week I was out of the hospital. I believe this was a miracle healing because the doctors said that most people in that condition died. I thanked God for giving me a second chance to be with my children.

This event turned my lifestyle around and changed the person I was. Before this, I used to spend a lot of hours at work; I worked over the weekends and virtually never spent quality time with my children. That changed, and to this day, I have become very protective over them and we spend time talking over everything. We became very close to each other, and most parents would probably feel the same. Most of the challenging decisions I have taken have been influenced by this new character. I made them with my children's future in mind and involved them in the decision making.

I would say I am loyal to what I am focused on. I am not really submissive. I am more outspoken and fight for the rights of those around me. Sometimes I do this directly or indirectly depending on the circumstances.

I am also a caring person, and I do not assume that these qualities come naturally just because one is a mother or a wife, I believe they might do so to a degree, but when cares of the world are overbearing, we sometimes come short of caring and that is where I had reached before that particular event occurred. I tended to focus on the provision of their material needs more than my giving myself as a person to them. I also take my feminine roles very seriously. However, I do not let this take the better part of me, I still pursue my goals.

I am very flexible both professionally and in my personal life. Professionally there are times when I have managed to take other responsibilities in other departments when called upon. I have volunteered in other instances, and also taken wide strides like travelling overseas on official duty whenever duty called.

I am very courageous, such that I have lived in different parts of the world even daring to do so in places where I knew no one previously. I often took my kids to adventurous drives just for the sake of it. We have been to Munich, Denmark, Nuernburg, Wurzburg. I believe we will still have many more places to go just for the fun of it.

One's character can be influenced by experiences and affiliations, but I believe that events that touch our souls bear more impact upon us. I have been changed for the better, and I believe that my children appreciate the change they see in me today because they have told me so. Each one of us should learn to cherish the company of those close to us it is fulfilling and satisfying to have quality time with those of our household.

Well, going back a little. When I came out of the hospital as usual money was scarce despite having given Charles both my two salaries and authority to operate my bank account. I reported back to the office, after a week's recuperation, there were mails I had to attend to immediately. Among them was my Bank Statement. I opened it and looked at it, something struck me, the account number was not mine, it was a current account (I operated a savings account) and it was a loan of US $20.000, however the name was mine. I sat up straight and thought to myself, I don't have a loan with the bank. I had been sick and my hospital bill had been cleared by my insurance that I had at work. I thought what an incredible mistake, how could a National bank make such a mistake? They had the right name, and address but wrong information?

I was furious. At around midday Charles came to see me and I shared this information with him. Immediately, I think I saw him shaken, he excused himself and went out shortly, (thinking back now, I guess he wanted time to brace himself on how to come and talk to me). A few minutes later he came back to the office and asked me to walk him out of the office. Once outside he said,

"I think I know about the issue with the bank."

"What?" I almost jumped out of my skin. I could not believe my ears.

"Did you take a loan from my bank using my name?" I asked.

"No, I'll explain this later." he said.

In the evening, when I asked about the bank issue, it was not easy for him to give me an explanation. What he told me was a line I had heard several times before whenever he had swindled money from anywhere.

He said, "Honey, actually whatever I have done is really going to help us and you will see a great change."

"Did you use my fixed deposit certificate?" I asked.

There was silence.

Till today, Charles never accepted or told me exactly what he did or what happened. I got so fed up of asking him to explain until one day I decided to find out what was going on at the bank. On reaching the bank, the two ladies I always talked to told me how sorry they were to learn about my sickness, and they were very sympathetic.

That struck me, how on earth did they know of my sickness? When I asked them how they knew, the news struck me like a bombshell.

"But your husband came here and was asking for a loan to help clear your hospital bill and we gave him since we know you and know him too." one of them said.

I demanded more information. The banker brought me my security file with all the necessary documents. My fixed deposit certificate was there attached- Charles had actually capitalized on my sickness and stole my certificate for his own evil motives.

My mind went racing, while, I lay dying someone calling himself my husband was busy planning how to cone his way to my savings. A letter he had written on my behalf and a forged signature was attached. They said that he had told them that I had been so sick to write the letter so he wrote it and that I had just signed it. I did not have any more strength, or words. I was angry not at him this time around but at myself, I should stop this from happening. My life cannot go on like this. How was I going to live with him again through all these, when it looks like he looks for every little opportunity to hurt me? I thought he was sick, actually demon possessed. Till this day, he has not paid the loan; it is not his loan according to the records but mine. It accumulated large amounts of interest that took up all my savings. My final word to him was I was not paying this debt for him this time around. Even if it meant going to court, I had had enough.

Please God help me. The painful part of it was the way I had saved the money that I had kept in this fixed deposit. I had denied myself the luxuries of good clothes, shoes and anything that goes with being a beautiful woman while in Germany, just to save. I had intended to use it to mortgage our first house. I cried to God, asking Him to show me how I could possibly live through all these, for me it was over. I wondered what it was that held me to him.

The following Sunday, I went to church and informed our pastor that I needed a divorce; however I never pursued it further than that. The problem was that he did not want me to take the children. I did not care much about him anymore. My question was did God intend that I suffer with a man like this? I did not even think I wanted to live with any man at all, was it not true that they were all the same? If I was to re-marry who knows, I may end up with the same kind of a person or even worse. Never, in my married life, did I have the experience of being a wife cared for by my husband. I only knew to struggle as though I was a single parent. There really was no difference between me and a widow with two children. What could I do to get away from him?

"Mhh" that is quite a tale, so what are you going to do about the situation?" Carolina asked.

I do not know that is why I am talking to you" I answered.

"What has the Lord been telling you? Have you listened to Him, I mean to the Spirit of the Lord within you?" Carolina asked.

"What do you mean?" I asked and after a second thought added, you mean to say God's Spirit has been talking to me all these years?"

"Exactly, that is what I mean" Carolina replied. When I did not say anything she went on "You know that is what happens, the word of God says for as many as are led by the Spirit, they are the sons of God. His Spirit within us always leads us as children and sons of God. However, most times we are either busy hearing other voices outside or we are just denying that He is actually speaking to us, sometimes we fear to act thinking that we might be acting out of flesh. The word says the Spirit Himself bears witness with our spirit."

She posed long enough to let it sink in. Then she went on, "So going back to my question, what has the Spirit of the Lord been telling you?"

"Well, if you mean what has been witnessing to my spirit. For a long period, I have felt there is no relationship. To me Charles has not been a husband in the real sense but a burden, an instrument of the enemy to keep me back. If I make two steps progress he pushes me back four steps." I answered.

So are you going to be obedient and obey the Voice or you are going to hold on to the marriage? Carolina's forthcoming boldness caught me unprepared. No one ever spoke to me so directly about my marriage. When I talked to my mother, all I had was sugar coated words of comfort that it would be alright. But this, I was not prepared for. I thought that she would encourage me to stay.

So I said, "I will be very truthful to you. We both came from backgrounds of one marriage with no divorce. Our traditional culture does not even think of divorce. Women are married to the community not only to the individual man. Apart from that, our Christian background is something you are aware of. So this is a difficult decision to make. If I do, what will the society think of me, what about my own mother, or my in-laws? What of the children?"

When Carolina said nothing, I went on. "Of late God has been dealing with me. I keep on opening the book of 1Samuel, 16:1 which says,

"And the Lord said unto Samuel, How long wilt thou mourn
for Saul, seeing I have rejected him from reigning over Israel?
Fill thine horn with oil and go, I will send thee to Jesse
the Bethlehemite: for I have provided me a King
among his sons."

This has been bothering me. But talking of the Spirit of the Lord bearing witness with my Spirit, each time I open this scripture, my spirit picks it up that this is referring to Charles and me. I feel that God is actually asking me how long I will mourn or keep up with Charles?"

"Then, what are you waiting for?"

"You mean I just go ahead and divorce?"

Remember, you are to hearken diligently unto the voice of the word of God and to observe to do all his commandments, obedience always brings the blessing, disobedience the curses.

"Oh God help me! Help me!"